1 MONTH OF
FREE
READING

at

www.ForgottenBooks.com

By purchasing this book you are eligible for one month membership to ForgottenBooks.com, giving you unlimited access to our entire collection of over 1,000,000 titles via our web site and mobile apps.

To claim your free month visit:

www.forgottenbooks.com/free916910

ISBN 978-0-266-96748-4
PIBN 10916910

LA SALLE
COLLEGE
PHILADELPHIA 41, PA.

CONDUCTED BY THE BROTHERS
OF THE CHRISTIAN SCHOOLS
SUPPLEMENT
1944-1945

ACCREDITED BY

Pennsylvania State Department of Public Instruction
The Middle States Association of Colleges and Secondary
*   Schools.*
Regents of the University of the State of New York.
The American Medical Association.
Pennsylvania State Board of Law Examiners.

MEMBER OF

The American Council on Education.
The Association of American Colleges.
The National Catholic Educational Association.
College and University Council of Pennsylvania.
The Association of Liberal Arts Colleges of Pennsylvania
*   the Advancement of Teaching.*
Pennsylvania Catholic Education Association.
Pennsylvania State Education Association.
American Library Association.
Educational Conference of the Brothers of the Christian Scho
American Catholic Historical Society.

INDIVIDUAL FACULTY MEMBERSHIP
IN LEARNED SOCIETIES

Eastern Association of Deans and Advisers of Men.
American Association of Collegiate Registrars.
American Association for the Advancement of Science.
American Chemical Society.
American Association of University Professors.
American Academy of Political and Social Sciences.
Classical Association of Atlantic States.
American Catholic Philosophical Association.
Association of College Presidents of Pennsylvania.
American Classical League.
American Economic Association.
Society of the Sigma Xi.
Botanical Society of Pennsylvania.
American Genetical Association.
Explorers' Club.
Genetics Society of America.
Pi Gamma Mu (Social Science) Fraternity.
American Catholic Sociological Society.
Catholic Economic Association

H

Officers and Faculty

FACULTY OF THE COLLEGE

BROTHER EMILIAN JAMES, F.S.C., D.Ped., LL.D.
President of the College

BROTHER G. LEWIS, F.S.C.
M.A. (Pennsylvania), Sc.D. (Duquesne)
Fellow, A.A.A.S.
Vice-President of the College
Professor of Mathematics

BROTHER G. PAUL, F.S.C.
M.S. (Catholic University), Ph.D. (Catholic University)
Dean of the College
Assistant Professor of Chemistry
Adviser to Alumni Association

BROTHER E. FELIX, F.S.C.
M.A. (Catholic University), D.F.A. (La Salle), Ph.D. (Fordham)
Director of Religious Instruction
Professor of Education and Philosophy

BROTHER E. ABDON, F.S.C.
M.A. (Pennsylvania)
Professor of German

BROTHER E. CHARLES, F.S.C.
M.A. (Catholic University), Sc.D. (Duquesne)
Professor of Chemistry

BROTHER E. PIUS, F.S.C.
M.A. (Rock Hill), Litt.D. (La Salle)
Professor of French

BROTHER FELICIAN PATRICK, F.S.C.
M.A. (La Salle), Ph.D. (Fordham), Litt.D. (Villanova)
Professor of English

ROLAND HOLROYD
M.A. (Pennsylvania), Ph.D. (Pennsylvania), Sc.D. (La Salle)
Fellow, A.A.A.S.
Professor of Biology

BROTHER G. ALPHONSUS, F.S.C.*
M.S. (Pennsylvania)
Professor of Comparative Anatomy and Embryology

BROTHER G. LEONARD, F.S.C.
M.A. (Rock Hill)
Professor of Political Science

* Absent on leave.

BROTHER G. JOSEPH, F.S.C.
M.A. (Rock Hill)
Registrar of the College
Professor of Physics

BROTHER EMILIAN PHILIP, F.S.C.*
Ph.D. (Fordham)
Professor of Philosophy and Psychology

BROTHER D. THOMAS, F.S.C.
M.A. (Catholic University), Ph.D. (Catholic University)
Associate Professor of Latin and Greek

BROTHER E. LUKE, F.S.C.
M.A.(Catholic University)
Associate Professor of English

JAMES J. HENRY
B.S. (Villanova), M.A. (Villanova)
Associate Professor of Finance and Business Law
Director of Athletics
Public Relations Officer

BROTHER E. LOUIS, F.S.C.
A.M. (Pennsylvania)
Assistant Professor of Spanish

BROTHER E. IGNATIUS, F.S.C.
M.A. (Pennsylvania)
Librarian

BROTHER D. AUGUSTINE, F.S.C.
M.A. (Catholic University), Ph.D. (Catholic University)
Assistant Professor of Sociology

BROTHER G. JOHN, F.S.C.*
Assistant Professor of Physics and Mathematics

JOSEPH F. FLUBACHER
A.B. (La Salle), M.A. (Temple)
Assistant Professor of Economics

BROTHER F. CHRISTOPHER, F.S.C.*
M.S. (Catholic University), Ph.D. (Catholic University)
Assistant Professor of Biology

* Absent on leave.

LA SALLE COLLEGE

BROTHER D. FRANCIS, F.S.C.
A.B. (La Salle), M.L. (Pittsburgh)
Instructor in Accounting

JOHN T. TOBIN
B.S. (La Salle)
Instructor in Accounting

BROTHER F. ALOYSIUS, F.S.C.
M.A. (La Salle), M.S. (Fordham), LL.D. (St. Francis)
Moderator of Athletics

JOHN GUISCHARD *
A.B. (La Salle), M.A. (Villanova)
Assistant Professor of French

REV. EDWARD J. CURRAN
M.A. (La Salle), LL.D. (La Salle)
College Historian

REV. DANIEL J. KANE, C.M.
College Chaplain

JOSEPH J. MEEHAN
B.S. (La Salie)
Athletics

GEORGE C. KIEFFER, M.D., Sc.D.
College Physician

* Absent on leave.

[6]

General Information

CALENDAR

·1945

January	3	Registration for Spring Term
January	31	Fall Term ends
February	7	Spring Term begins
May	16	Registration for Summer Term
June	1	Spring Term ends

ENTRANCE REQUIREMENTS

Students who completed the course of studies of any senior high school approved by the State Department of Public Instruction of Pennsylvania are eligible for matriculation at La Salle College. Students who rank in the first or second quintile of the graduating class are admitted without examination; all others must take entrance examinations.

During the emergency, the Department of Public Instruction of the State of Pennsylvania, permits a student who has completed three and a half years of high school to enter college, provided:

a. The student ranks near the top of his class.

b. The high school Principal judges the student capable of doing college work.

Prospective students should file their applications early. Application blanks may be obtained from the Registrar upon request.

Transcripts of high school records should be mailed as soon as possible, by the high school Principal to the Committee on Admissions. Forms for this purpose are furnished on application to the Registrar.

HEALTH CERTIFICATE

Each candidate for admission to the College must present a health certificate signed by a physician and attesting to the physical ability of the applicant to carry college work.

PHYSICAL EDUCATION

All students must follow the Physical Fitness Program. The Program is designed to provide:

1. A type of Physical activity to condition all the students.

2. Physical activity which will accomplish well rounded fitness and progressive development.

3. A stimulating effect on participants, and create a desire in them to keep physically fit.

Courses Leading to the Degree of Bachelor of Arts

A candidate for any of the courses leading to the degree of Bachelor of Arts. must have fifteen high school units distributed as follows:

English .... 3 units (four years)
American History .... 1 unit
Algebra (Quadratics included) .... 1 unit
Plane Geometry .... 1 unit
Language* .... 2 units
Science .... 1 unit

Six additional units will be accepted from the following: Latin, History, French, Mathematics. Spanish, Economics, German, Sociology, Physics, Problems in Democracy, Civics, Chemistry, Biology, Physiology and Hygiene, General Science.

Courses Leading to the Degree of Bachelor of Science

A candidate for the degree of Bachelor of Science . must have fifteen high school units distributed as follows:

English .... 3 units (four years)
American History .... 1 unit
Mathematics .... 1 unit
Language* .... 2 units
Science ....:............. 1 unit

Seven additional units will be selected from the general list of requirements for the Bachelor of Arts degree.

Students entering for the courses in Business Administration, who offer Business Law, Bookkeeping, Drawing and most commercial subjects, may receive credit but not for Typewriting, Penmanship or Physical Education.

In foreign languages two units of the same language are required.

ADVANCED STANDING

Credits from other colleges are accepted towards advanced standing in courses having a certifying grade, provided such courses are listed in the La Salle College catalogue. Such entrants shall be required to make up the prescribed subjects of study in the course which they wish to pursue. Results of tests and examinations directed by the United States Armed Forces Institute will be considered for credit by La Salle. A complete record of the subjects studied must be mailed by the proper college officer to the Committee on Standing before any action on the status of the student will be taken.

REQUIREMENTS FOR THE DEGREE OF BACHELOR OF ARTS

La Salle College offers several courses leading to the degree of Bachelor of Arts. These courses meet the needs of those desiring a liberal education and prepare for the professions.

Summary of Requirements for the Bachelor of Arts degree:

1. Successful completion of a course in Religion (Catholic students) or Ethics (non-Catholic students) is required of all students.

2. Quantitative requirements; 128 semester hours.

3. Qualitative requirements; 128 quality points.

4. A senior comprehensive examination in the Major subject.

5. At least seventy-five per cent of the quantitative requirements, and also of the qualitative requirements must be earned in subjects listed in Groups I, II and IV, page 21.

6. A Major is defined as 24 semester hours credit in one subject and 12 semester hours credit in a closely related subject.

REQUIREMENTS FOR THE DEGREE OF BACHELOR OF SCIENCE

The College offers in the School of Business Administration two courses leading to the degree of Bachelor of Science:

1. Bachelor of Science in Business Administration.

2. Bachelor of Science in Accounting.

The Religion, Quantitative and Qualitative requirements for the degree of Bachelor of Science are the same as for the degree of Bachelor of Arts. Other requirements:

3. A senior comprehensive examination in the Major subject.

4. A Major subject, as defined in number 6 above, must be selected from Groups two and three. More complete information will be found in the "Agenda."

MAJORS AND MINORS

The various courses of instruction are divided into four groups as follows:

Group I.	Group II.
English	Economics
Ethics	Education
French	History
German	Political Science
Greek	Sociology
Latin	
Philosophy	
Spanish	

Group III.	Group IV.
Accounting	Biology
Business Law	Chemistry
Finance	Mathematics
Insurance	Physics

All the work of the Senior Year must be performed in residence at La Salle College.

GENERAL REGULATIONS

REGISTRATION FOR COURSES

1. Registration for the year 1944-1945 must be made by February 12, 1945, June 18, 1945.

   Freshmen are required to be on the campus three days before the upper classmen report. The student consults with an Adviser or with the Dean or Registrar regarding his curriculum. He takes the necessary tests, learns about the extra-curricular activities from their respective representatives, and in general becomes acquainted with the College, the Faculty members, and other members of his Class and undergoes medical examination.

2. No student will be admitted to any class until he has registered at the Registrar's office and received his card of admittance. This must be presented at every class upon request of the teacher.

3. A student will not be allowed to change from one Course to another after the first week of the term. By "Course" is meant the general summary of a group of subjects leading to a degree, such as Education, Accounting, etc.

4. If a student wishes to change from one course to another, he may do so only with the approval of the Dean of the College. The request, with reasons therefor must be made in writing. Any necessary subjects which the student may lack for the new course must be made up.

5. Students who wish to change or drop subjects in a course may do so only with the written permission of the Dean. Such arrangements must be made during the first week of the term.

6. A student is required to complete the introductory and preliminary subjects of a Department before being admitted to the advanced subjects of that Department.

7. Students may not register for more than eighteen semester hours of credit work without the permission of the Dean.

EXAMINATIONS, GRADES, CREDITS

15. Term examinations for credit are held at the end of January, May and September. Mid-Term tests are made at the end of November, March and July.

16. The college uses the Quality Point Grading system. In this system the first five letters of the alphabet serve as the grades and are evaluated by points according to the following scale:

    A—Superior—93-100—3 quality points for each credit hour.

    B—High—84-92—2 quality points for each credit hour.

    C—Average—77-83—1 quality point for each credit hour.

    D—Barely Passing—70-76—0 quality points.

    F—Failure.

17. A credit or semester hour is defined as one hour of lecture or two hours of laboratory work a week for one term.

20. A bulletin, based on the class work and the examinations, is sent to parents or guardians at the end of each term.

21. If at the end of any term, a student has grades less than "D" in one half of the credit hours of that term, he shall be asked to withdraw.

22. No reports, diplomas, certificates or other scholastic information will be given to the student whose financial account with the college has not been settled in full.

23. A student will be considered as a member of the lowest class of which he has not fully satisfied the requirements.

ATTENDANCE

30. The scholastic year of the College consists of two terms. The term consists of sixteen weeks and is the unit of credit.

31. Classes begin at 8:30 A. M.

32. Excuses for absence from class will not be accepted if delivered over the telephone.

33. If in any term the number of absences in any subject exceeds twice the number of credit hours in that subject, the student may not return to that class. For instance, if the number of credit hours is three, a student must discontinue the course when he has seven absences without legitimate reason. In sciences requiring laboratory work, the number of credit hours for lecture and laboratory are considered separately. If, for good reason, the Dean and the Professor concerned permit his continuance, he shall not be rated higher than "D" in the subject for that term.

34. Classes missed by a student at the beginning of a term count against him in the same manner as other absences.

MISCELLANEOUS

35. If a student withdraws from the College during the scholastic year he should notify the Registrar.

36. Students should report promptly to the office of the Registrar and that of the Bursar any change of address on his own part or that of his parents or guardian.

37. A course will not be offered unless the number of applicants is sufficient to warrant the interest and effort involved.

DEAN'S HONOR LIST

After the completion of each set of term examinations, a student who receives rating of not less than "B" in every subject required by his course will be placed upon the Dean's Honor List and will be designated as an Honor Student. He must have complied, also, with the disciplinary regulations of the College. Honor upper-classmen are exempted from the regulations which refer to attendance in all subjects except Religion. Honor students forfeit their titles and privileges if they receive an "F" in any subject at the mid-term tests.

HONORS AT GRADUATION

A candidate for the Bachelor degree who has an average of 3.8 in all required subjects in the first seven terms of his college course will be designated as "MAXIMA CUM LAUDE"; "MAGNA CUM LAUDE," for those who receive a 3.5 average; "CUM LAUDE" for those who have 3.2 average. (Numerical equivalents of grades to be used in computing honors average: A-4; B-3; C-2; D-1.)

FINANCIAL REGULATIONS

Tuition—Payments for each term must be made during registration week. Registration is not complete until the Bursar's receipt is obtained for an approved schedule of studies. No refund will be made except in the case of protracted illness.

Scholarships—Scholarship holders must maintain a "B" average.

Books, fees, and other items are not included in any scholarship.

Class Requisites—Books, stationery and other class requisites must be paid for when the purchase is made at the book store of the College.

Student Property—The College will not be responsible for books and other property belonging to the student while in his keeping nor for any such property left at the College.

EXPENSES

Tuition, term $150.00*

Student Activities Fee (payable by all students). This
fee includes subscription to student publications,
athletic privileges, intramural sports, examination
supplies and library fees.

Autumn term	25.00
Spring term	25.00
Summer term	15.00

Sciences

Regular term	10.00
Accelerated Courses	20.00

Visual Education (Seniors in Education) 5.00

Breakage Deposit Fee (Chemistry) 5.00

Microscope (Biology)

Regular term	5.00
Accelerated Courses	10.00

Religious Activities, term 5.00

Matriculation Fee (Payable only once) 5.00

Late Registration Fee 5.00

Delayed Examination Fee (For each subject) .. .., 1.00

Additional Transcript of Record (In advance) 2.00

Graduation Fee 25.00

*Graduates of some Catholic High Schools are
eligible for scholarship grants of $50.00 per term.

Tuition and Fees when paid on the Installment Plan are
subject to a carrying charge fee of $5.00 per term.

Curricula

BACHELOR OF ARTS
Classics and Philosophy

FRESHMAN LEVEL

Ethics 1	6-4
English 1A-1B-3-14	8-8
Modern Languages 1A-1B	6-6
or 2-3	6-6
Latin 8-18	6-6
History 11	4-4
Biology 2	8-6
Mathematics 1-2	6-6
Physical Education	3

SOPHOMORE LEVEL

Ethics 2	6-4
English 4-12	4-4
Modern Language 2-3	6-6
or 4-5	4-4
Philosophy 2-14	6-6
Latin 19 or 20	6-6
Greek 1	6-6
Sociology 1	3-3
Physical Education	3

JUNIOR LEVEL

Ethics 3	6-4
English 8-20	4-4
Modern Languages 4-5	4-4
Greek 2-4	6-6
Latin 15	3-3
Sociology 4	2-2
Philosophy 1A-1B-7	9-9
Electives	3
Physical Education	3

SENIOR LEVEL

Ethics 4	6-4
English 5-19	4-4
Latin 9 or 12, 13	6-6
Philosophy 13A-13B	6-6
Sociology 3-5	4-4
History 20	4-4
Electives	12
Physical Education	3

BACHELOR OF ARTS
Education

FRESHMAN LEVEL

Ethics 1	6-4
English 1A-1B-3-14	8-8
Molern Languages 1A-1B	6-6
or 2-3	6-6
History 14 or 15, 23	8-8
Mathematics 1-2	6-6
Biology 2	8-6
Physical Education	3

SOPHOMORE LEVEL

Ethics 2	6-4
English 4-12	4-4
Modern Languages 2-3	6-6
or 4-5	4-4
Philosophy 2-7-14	9-9
History 15 or 14	4-4
Education 17	3-3
Sociology 1	3-3
Economics 11	6-6
Physical Education	3

JUNIOR LEVEL

Ethics 3	6-4
English 8-20	4-4
Modern Languages 4-5	4-4
Philosophy 1A-1B	6-6
Education 3-14-15	9-9
History 20	4-4
Sociology 4	2-2
Political Science 1	6-6
Physical Education	3

SENIOR LEVEL

Ethics 4	6-4
English 5	2-2
Education 2-5-7-8-11-12	16-16
Philosophy 13A	3-3
Electives	9
Physical Education	3

NOTE: The first column denotes the number of clock-hours and the second column denotes the number of credit hours.

BACHELOR OF ARTS
Preparation for Law

FRESHMAN LEVEL

Ethics 1	6-4
English 1A-1B-3-14	8-8
Modern Languages 1A-1B	6-6
or 2-3	6-6
Mathematics 1-2	6-6
History 14 or 15	4-4
Biology 2	8-6
Business Law 1	3-3
Physical Education	3

JUNIOR LEVEL

Ethics 3	6-4
English 8-20	4-4
Business Law 3-4	6-6
Sociology 4	2-2
History 13	4-4
Economics 12-22	8-8
Modern Languages 4-5	4-4
Political Science 1	6-6
Philosophy 7	3-3
Physical Education	3

SOPHOMORE LEVEL

Ethics 2	6-4
English 4-12	4-4
Modern Languages 2-3	6-6
or 4-5	4-4
Philosophy 2-14	6-6
History 15 or 14	4-4
Business Law 2	3-3
Sociology 1	3-3
Economics 11	6-6
Physical Education	3

SENIOR LEVEL

Ethics 4	6-4
History 16-20	8-8
Sociology 3-5	4-4
Philosophy 1A-1B	6-6
Political Science 3-4	4-4
Finance 3	4-4
Electives	6
Physical Education	3

BACHELOR OF ARTS
Pure Science

FRESHMAN LEVEL

Ethics 1	6-4
English 1A-1B-3-14	8-8
Modern Languages 1A-1B	6-6
or 2-3	6-6
Mathematics 1-2	6-6
Chemistry 1	10-8
Biology 2	8-6
Physical Education	3

JUNIOR LEVEL

Ethics 3	6-4
English 8-20	4-4
Modern Languages 4-5	4-4
Sociology 4	2-2
Mathematics 7-10	6-6
Philosophy 2	3-3
Chemistry 1-16A-16B	22-15
Physical Education	3

SOPHOMORE LEVEL

Ethics 2	6-4
English 4-12	4-4
Modern Languages 2-3	6-6
or 4-5	4-4
Mathematics 4-6	6-6
Physics 1	10-8
Chemistry 2-4	11-7
Sociology 1	3-3
Physical Education	3

SENIOR LEVEL

Ethics 4	6-4
Philosophy 1A-1B-7	9-9
Electives *	23
Physics	
Chemistry	
Mathematics	
Physical Education	3
* Ten credits for Electives to be chosen from Groups I-II.	

Note: The first column denotes the number of clock-hours and the second column denotes the number of credit hours.

BACHELOR OF ARTS
Preparation for Medicine

FRESHMAN LEVEL
Ethics 1	6-4
English 1A-1B-3-14	8-8
Modern Languages 1A-1B	6-6
or 2-3	6-6
Mathematics 1-2	6-6
Chemistry 1	10-8
Biology 2	8-6
Physical Education	3

JUNIOR LEVEL
Ethics 3	6-4
Modern Languages 4-5	4-4
or 6-7	4-4
Philosophy 2-7-14	9-9
Sociology 4	2-2
English 8-20	4-4
Biology 3-7-12	9-7
Chemistry 3	10-8
Physical Education	3

SOPHOMORE LEVEL
Ethics 2	6-4
English 4-12	4-4
Modern Languages 2-3	6-6
or 4-5	4-4
Biology * 1-4	14-10
Physics 1	10-8
Chemistry * 2-4	11-7
Sociology 1	3-3
Physical Education	3

SENIOR LEVEL
Ethics 4	6-4
Philosophy 1A-1B	6-6
Sociology 5	2-2
Biology 5-6-11	12-8
Chemistry 5-6	12-8
Modern Languages 6-7	4-4
Physical Education	3

* With the permission of the Dean, Pre-Dental students may substitute Biology 3 for Biology 1 and Chemistry 3 for Chemistry 2-4.

BACHELOR OF SCIENCE
Business Administration

FRESHMAN LEVEL
Ethics 1	6-4
English 1A-1B-3-14	8-8
Modern Languages 1A-1B	6-6
or 2-3	6-6
Accounting 1	6-6
Mathematics 1-2	6-6
Business Law 1	3-3
History 23	4-4
Physical Education	3

JUNIOR LEVEL
Ethics 3	6-4
English 4-12	4-4
Modern Languages 4-5	4-4
Insurance 1	5-5
Business Law 3-4	6-6
Economics 12	4-4
Finance 2	4-4
Philosophy 2-14	6-6
Political Science 1	6-6
Physical Education	3

SOPHOMORE LEVEL
Ethics 2	6-4
English 30	4-4
Modern Languages 2-3	6-6
or 4-5	4-4
Business Law 2	3-3
Finance 1	6-6
Economics 11-22	10-10
Sociology 1	3-3
Physical Education	3

SENIOR LEVEL
Ethics 4	6-4
English 8-20	4-4
Sociology 3-4	4-4
Political Science 3-4	4-4
Economics 15 or 17	4-4
Philosophy 1A-1B	6-6
History 20	4-4
Finance 3	4-4
Physical Education	3

NOTE: The first column denotes the number of clock-hours and the second column denotes the number of credit hours.

[20]

BACHELOR OF SCIENCE
Accounting

FRESHMAN LEVEL

Ethics 1	6-4
English 1A-1B-3-14	8-8
Modern Languages 1A-1B	6-6
or 2-3	6-6
Accounting 1	6-6
Mathematics 1-2	6-6
Business Law 1	3-3
History 23	4-4
Physical Education	3

SOPHOMORE LEVEL

Ethics 2	6-4
English 30	4-4
Modern Languages 2-3	6-6
or 4-5	4-4
Business Law 2	3-3
Finance 1	6-6
Economics 11-22	10-10
Accounting 2	6-6
Physical Education	3

JUNIOR LEVEL

Ethics 3	6-4
Modern Languages 4-5	4-4
Accounting 3-4	10-8
Insurance 1	5-5
Business Law 3-4	6-6
Sociology 1	3-3
Finance 2	4-4
Philosophy 2-14	6-6
Physical Education	3

SENIOR LEVEL

Ethics 4	6-4
Sociology 4	2-2
Accounting 5-6-7	14-12
Philosophy 1A-1B	6-6
History 20	4-4
Finance 3	4-4
English 4	2-2
Physical Education	3

NOTE: The first column denotes the number of clock-hours and the second column denotes the number of credit hours.

Departments

ACCOUNTING

BROTHER D. FRANCIS, F.S.C., M.L.
JOHN T. TOBIN, B.S.

1. *Introduction to Accounting.*—A thorough training in the fundamental principles and practice of recording business transactions; presenting and interpreting the financial facts of a business which includes sole proprietorship, partnership and corporations.

(6 hours, 1 term.)

2. *Advanced Accounting.*—Capital and Revenue; All forms of Working Papers; A thorough analysis of Corporation Accounting, as to Stock Issues, Capital and Net Worth; Special treatment of Cash and the other Current Assets, also the Current Liabilities; Inventories, as to Kinds and Price; Consignments; Installments; Valuation of Fixed Assets; Advantages and Disadvantages of Fixed Liabilities; Funds and Reserves; Comparative Statements; Analysis of Working Capital; Profit and Loss Analysis and the Application of Funds; the mathematies of investment.

(6 hours, 1 term.)

3. *Cost Accounting.*—Discussion of the necessity, importance and place of cost accounting in modern enterprises; the control of stores; purchasing and issuing, the running inventory; quality, remuneration, and control of labor, methods of distributing overhead expenses or "burden" and their limitations; calculation of machine-rates; waste and leakage in factories; idle time; forms used in different "job and process" costing systems; budget control; the installation and operation of systems of standard costs. Prerequisites, Accounting 1, 2.

(3 hours lecture, 2 hours laboratory, 1 term.)

4. *Auditing.*—Underlying principles. The duties and liabilities of accountants and auditors; qualifications and the canons of professional ethics. Practical instruction as to the purpose and conduct of the audit; detection of fraud and defalcations; discussion of methods of internal check and the detection of fraud. Prerequisites, Accounting 1, 2.

(3 hours lecture, 2 hours laboratory, 1 term.)

5. *Practical Accounting Systems.*—Application of principles to accounting systems of various types of businesses; building and loan associations; insurance companies; banks; department stores, public utilities, and railroads; the principles underlying revenue and expense and fund systems of accounts as applied to the records of municipalities. Prerequisites, Accounting 1, 2.

(3 hours lecture, 2 hours laboratory, 1 term.)

6. *Certified Public Accountant Course.*—Mergers; consolidated statements and balance sheets; holding corporations; partnership adjustments; accounts of executors and trustees and law involved; insolvency in connection with realization and liquidation. Prerequisite, senior rating.

(3 hours lecture, 2 hours laboratory, 1 term.)

7. *Accounting. Federal and State Taxes.*—A detailed study of Federal and State tax laws, regulations, and returns. Particular emphasis is placed on the following: Individual Rates; Credits, Income; Gain or Loss, Deductions, Inventories, Partnerships; Estates and Trusts, Corporations; Excess Profits Tax; Foreign Corporations; Reorganizations; Social Security; Estate and Gift Tax; Capital Stock Tax.

(4 hours, 1 term.)

BIOLOGY

Roland Holroyd, Ph.D.
Brother G. Alphonsus, F.S.C., M.S.
Brother F. Christopher, F.S.C., M.S., Ph.D.

1. *General Botany.*—An introductory course including:

    (a) A study of the form, structure and life processes of flowering plants.

    (b) Life-history studies in types of plant life: bacteria, algae, fungi, liverworts, mosses, ferns, cycads, conifers and the leading groups of angiosperms. Laboratory work is supplemented by plant analysis.

    (4 hours lecture, 4 hours laboratory, 1 term.)

2. *General Zoology.*—An introductory course dealing with the characteristics of living matter, cell structure, the com-

parative anatomy of leading phyla of animals, problems of heredity, etc., together with a review of significant animal types from the protozoa to the mammal.

(4 hours lecture, 4 hours laboratory, 1 term.)

3. *Mammalian Anatomy.*—The cat is used as a type of the higher mammal to familiarize the student with skeletal, muscular, vascular and nervous relationships together with their physiological interpretation. Prerequisite, Biology 2.

(1 hour lecture, 4 hours laboratory, 1 term.)

4. *Comparative Anatomy.*—A phylogenetic course embracing a comparative study of typical chordates from Amphioxus to the Aves. Prerequisite, Biology 2.

(2 hours lecture, 4 hours laboratory, 1 term.)

5. *Histology.*—The course is designed to acquaint the student with the minute structure of various tissues together with their relationships in the formation of organs. Prerequisites, Biology 3 and 11. For Juniors and Seniors only.

(2 hours lecture, 4 hours laboratory, 1 term.)

6. *Embryology.*—The fundamental processes underlying vertebrate development and differentiation are studied. The chick and pig form the basis of instruction. Prerequisites, Biology 5 and 11. For Seniors only.

(1 hour lecture, 2 hours laboratory, 1 term.)

7. *Bacteriology, An Introductory Course.*—A lecture-demonstration course concerned with the role of bacteria in nature and especially in human affairs. Prerequisite, Biology 1.

(2 hours lecture and demonstration, 1 term.)

11. *Biological Micro-Technique.*—Methods employed in the preparation of plant and animal tissues for microscopical study. Prerequisite, Biology 3.

(1 hour lecture, 2 hours laboratory, 1 term.)

12. *Organic Evolution and Genetics.*—A lecture course outlining briefly the history of the development of evolutionary thought and presenting the evidence for organic evolution together with the leading theories which have been advanced; the scope and method of genetics or modern experimental evolution; Mendel's law of heredity as applied to plants and animals. Prerequisite, Biology 1, 2, or 17. (2 hours lecture, 1 term.)

14. *Taxonomy of the Angiosperms.*—A study of the classification of seed plants. Practice in the use of identification keys. The Phylogeny and economic importance of the leading families of conifers and flowering plants will be emphasized. Two hours lecture, practical work or field excursion. Spring term. Two semester hours credit. Prerequisite, Biology 1 or 17.

15. *Horticultural and Forest Botany.*—The relation of man to cultivated plants. Soil, plant propagation, elements of landscape horticulture, etc., together with the basic problems of forestry. Two hours lecture supplemented by visits to greenhouses and botanic gardens. One term. Two semester hours credit. Prerequisite, Biology 1 or 17.

17. *General Biology.*—An introduction to the structure and metabolism of both the flowering plants and vertebrate animals. A survey of the plant and animal kingdoms. The laws of heredity as illustrated by plant and animal breeding. The history of biological thought.

(4 hours lecture and recitation, 4 hours laboratory, 1 term.)

18. *Systematic Biology.*—A study of the phylogenic development of plants and animals. Representative types of animals and plants are studied from the protozoa to the vertebrates and from the bacteria to the angiosperms. This course is the equivalent of and is taken in conjunction with the second semesters of Biology 1 and 2. Prerequisite, Biology 17.

(4 hours lecture, 4 hours laboratory, 1 term.)

21. *History of Biology.*—The early philosophical beginnings of the science and its subsequent development; the principal epochs; the rise of the "research method" and the present day fields of active biological investigation. Prerequisites, Senior standing and permission to register.   (2 hours lecture or seminar, 1 term.)

Seminar.—A seminar is conducted from time to time throughout the year to further the work of the department. All students in the biology courses are expected to participate.

BUSINESS LAW

James J. Henry, M.A.

1. *Law of Contracts.*—The study of Contracts and the Laws of Agency. Under Contracts, the formation of the contractual relation, operation, interpretation, and discharge. Under Agency, the formation, rights and duties of both the agent and principal, effect upon third parties and termination.
(3 hours, 1 term.)

2. *The Law of Business Association.*—This course includes the subjects of partnership and corporations. The law of partnership involves a study of the formation of a partnership; duties, rights, and authority of partners; liability of partners; dissolution of partnerships. The law of corporations includes, with special emphasis on the Business Corporation Code of Pennsylvania, creating corporations; corporate powers: membership; management; termination.
(3 hours, 1 term.)

3. *Personal and Real Property.*—Definition and classification of property. Acquisition and control of personal property. Bailments with particular reference to common carriers, innkeepers, and factors and warehousemen. The Uniform Sales Act. Acquisition and transfer of real property. Quantum of estates. Conveyancing, Mortgages. Landlord and Tenant.
(3 hours, 1 term.)

[27]

4. *Crimes—Decedents' Estates—Negotiable Instruments.*—
The criminal law in general with particular reference
to offenses against business relations and transactions.
Management of Decedents' Estates. The Intestate
Law. The Wills Act. The Uniform Negotiable Instru-
ments Law.

(3 hours, 1 term.)

CHEMISTRY

BROTHER E. CHARLES, F.S.C., M.A., Sc.D.
BROTHER G. PAUL, F.S.C., M.S., PH.D.

1. *General Chemistry.*—The Fundamental concepts, laws and
theories of chemistry are presented, and the quantitative aspects are emphasized by suitable calculations.
Proportionate time is devoted to the descriptive study
of some of the elements and their compounds.

(5 hours lecture, 1 hour recitation, 4 hours laboratory,
1 term.)

2-4. *Analytical Chemistry.*—A combined course in Qualitative
and Quantitative Analysis. The lecture topics treat of
atomic and molecular structure, conductivity, physical
and chemical equilibrium, electrochemistry and the
methods of Qualitative and Quantitative Analysis.
The laboratory experiments combine both Qualitative
and Quantitative techniques of analysis.

(3 hours lecture, 8 hours laboratory, 1 term.)

3. *Organic Chemistry.*—The principles of chemistry are ex-
tended and applied to the study of carbon compounds,
including both aliphatic and aromatic derivatives. In
the laboratory, typical organic compounds are prepared
and studied. Prerequisite, Chemistry 4.

(4 hours lecture, 8 hours laboratory, 1 term.)

5. *Physiological Chemistry.*—The study of the composition, reactions and products of living material together with a discussion of the carbohydrates, fats and proteins. In the laboratory, food-stuffs, blood, urine and digestive juices are studied and analyzed. Prerequisite, Chemistry 3.

   (2 hours lecture, 4 hours laboratory, 1 term.)

6. *Physical Chemistry.* (Pre-Medical Students)—The elementary theoretical principles applicable to all branches of chemistry are studied and illustrated, principally through the solution of numerous problems. Laboratory experiments to illustrate these principles are performed. Prerequisite, Chemistry 3.

   (2 hours lecture, 4 hours laboratory, 1 term.)

7. *Chemical History and Literature.*—Researches into the sources of information important to chemists and scientists in general. Numerous articles in chemical journals, both American and foreign, are to be read and reported on, in the form of essays.

   (2 hours, 1 term.)

8. *Advanced Quantitative Analysis.*—The principles of physical chemistry, as applied to the theory of quantitative analysis are presented. The laboratory work includes the calibration of apparatus, mineral analysis, and special methods of quantitative analysis, such as electrodeposition, conductimetric and potentiometric titrations, and colorimetric analysis.

   (Hours to be arranged.)

9. *Advanced Organic Chemistry.*—A comprehensive consideration of the general and specific methods of organic syntheses, together with the theoretical consideration of the structure and reactions of organic compounds.

   (Hours to be arranged.)

16. *Physical Chemistry.* (Pure Science Students). In the first term, the lecture topics are: The Structure of Matter; Liquids; Solutions; Thermochemistry; and Elementary

Thermodynamics. In the second term the topics are: Homogeneous and Heterogeneous Equilibria; Chemical Kinetics; Electrolytic Inductance; Electromotive Force; Chemical Thermodynamics.

Quantitative laboratory experiments are selected to illustrate most of the lecture topics.

(2 hours lecture, 1 hour problems, 3 hours laboratory, 2 terms).

ECONOMICS
JOSEPH F. FLUBACHER, M.A.

11. *Principles of Economics.*—A general introductory course designed to acquaint the student with fundamental economic principles and processes as they appear in such phenomena as production, exchange, value, distribution, consumption and public finance. Reports, readings, discussions and lectures. This course is a prerequisite for all other economics courses.

(6 hours, 1 term.)

12. *Economic Problems.*—Current economic problems of national life are analyzed and discussed in class. Typical problems are those of business organizations and markets, money and banking, trusts, railroads, international trade and tariff, taxation, labor problems, government ownership, economic planning. Reports, readings, discussions.

(4 hours, 1 term.)

15a. *History of Economic Thought.*—A detailed study of the development of the leading economic concepts. The contributions of the early philosophers, the Middle Ages, the Mercantilists, the Classicists and the Neo-Classicists are considered. (2 hours, 1 term.)

15b. *Contemporary Economic Movements.*—A continuation of Economics, 15a. Socialism, both Utopian and Scientific, is treated. A study of Communism is next made, followed by Fascism, its policies and effects. The economic and social effects of the Nazi Dictatorship; the social philosophy of Pope Leo XIII, and Pope Pius XI.

(2 hours, 1 term.)

17. *Industrial Relations and Labor Problems in America.*— Social and economic factors in industrial relations. Insecurity, inadequate income, work, sub-standard workers and industrial conflict. Labor unions are studied. Existing and proposed legislation and remedies are examined in detail. Emphasis is placed on the problem of unemployment. Reports, readings and class discussion. (Given in alternate years.)

(4 hours, 1 term.)

22a. *American Economic History.—The Colonial Age.*—The imperial frontier; production in the British colonies; the domain of colonial commerce. Agricultural conquest of the West; slavery; the agricultural revolution; the decline of foreign commerce; the rise of domestic commerce; markets and machines; the formation of a laboring class. (2 hours, 1 term.)

22b. *American Economic History.—The Industrial State.*—The railroad age; the development and use of natural resources; the farmer and the machine age; the wage earner under competition and monopoly; the revolt against big business. The imperial nation.

(2 hours, 1 term.)

EDUCATION
BROTHER E. FELIX, F.S.C., PH.D.

2. *Visual Education.*—Types of visual aids and values of each: the school journey or field trip; object—specimen—model and museum instruction; apparatus and equipment; still projectors and their attachments; motion pictures; pictorial material; standard visual equipment; visual aids and the curriculum; psychological background of visual education, and bibliography. (Given in alternate years.) (3 hours, 1 term.)

3. *Educational Psychology.*—A practical course applying the principles of psychology to educational methods. The acquisition of study habits is investigated. Problems

concerning learning, individual capacities and differences, and the transfer of training are studied. The value of interest, attention and memory is discussed. General psychology is a prerequisite.

(3 hours, 1 term.)

5. *Special Methods.*—This course investigates methods suitable to various courses of instruction. The aim of the course is to qualify prospective teachers to specialize in their chosen fields. (3 hours, 1 term.)

7. *History of Education.—Ancient and Medieval.*—The development of formal education from the earliest nations. A detailed study of leading characters; educational movements. Their effect on educational history. A comparison with modern thinkers and their views. Particular stress on Scholasticism and the Universities. (Given in alternate years.) (2 hours, 1 term.)

8. *History of Education—Modern.*—The story of education as it developed from mediaeval times to our own day. The outstanding educators who brought about this development. The spread of education in recent times, and a comparison of American education with European systems. Educational leaders and movements of today. (Given in alternate years.) (2 hours, 1 term.)

11. *Observation of Teaching.*—Students in their Senior year observe classroom procedure in approved high schools. Seminar meetings are held in which the notes and observations of the student teachers are discussed.

(90 clock hours, 1 term.)

12. *Practice Teaching.*—In conjunction with Education 11. Students have actual classroom experience by teaching in the regular class periods. This work is done under the supervision of the regular class teacher and includes all the details of class management. Critical reports of this work are forwarded by the head of the department to the Professor of Education.

(90 clock hours, 1 term.)

13. *Educational Measurements.*—An introduction to the nature, purpose and technique of modern testing in secondary schools. (2 hours, 1 term.)

14. *Principles of High School Teaching.*—This course includes the following topics: outcomes of teaching; questioning; assignments; planning the instruction; appreciation teaching; problem and project teaching; organization and procedure; drill lessons, visual aims; socialized class procedure; directed study; measuring the results of teaching; marks and marking; classroom routine.
(3 hours, 1 term.)

15. *Secondary Education.*—Principles of secondary education; physical and mental traits of high school pupils. Place and function of the public high school. Selection and organization of the study program.
(3 hours, 1 term.)

17. *Introduction to Education.*—A brief presentation of the development, meaning, scientific basis. methods and the. fundamental problems of instruction.
(3 hours, 1 term.)

ENGLISH

Brother Felician, F.S.C., Ph.D.
Brother E. Luke, F.S.C., M.A.

Courses 1 and 14 are prerequisites for all English courses excepting 3.

0. *Remedial English.*—Required of all Freshmen who fail to attain a satisfactory mark in the special English examination at the beginning of the first term. The course embraces intensive practice in the fundamentals of English grammar and composition which a College student should have at his command.

1. *Prose Composition.* (2 hours, 2 terms.)

3. *Public Speaking.*—The fundamentals of speech composition.
(1 hour, 2 terms.)

4. *American Literature.*—A survey of the literature of America from Colonial Times to the present day.
(2 hours, 1 term.)

5. *Literary Criticism.*—A study of the fundamental principles of literature and style; practice in construction; reports on assigned readings; applications of principles of literary criticism to American and English authors.
(2 hours, 1 term.)

8. *Shakespeare.*—A study of Shakespeare, poet, dramatist, and man; his sources, the transmission of his text, and other problems growing out of the reading of six selected plays, the poems, and critical appraisals.
(2 hours, 1 term.)

12. *The English Novel.*—A survey of the growth of the novel in England from its origins in the early romances to the beginning of the present century.
(2 hours, 1 term.)

13. *Philosophy of Literature.*—Origin and function of literature; influencing agencies in literature; characteristics of ancient and modern literature. The literary artist.
(2 hours, 1 term.)

14. *A Survey of English Literature.*—An outline of the development of the literature of England by periods.
(1 hour, 2 terms.)

19. *Twentieth Century Literature.*—Present-day literary movements and conditions in America, England, and Continental Europe. Lectures, readings, and discussions.
(2 hours, 1 term.)

20. *English Poetry.*—A study of poetic types; the meaning and purpose of poetry; the laws of English prosody. Emphasis on the aesthetic experience and the creative process. Reading will include poets of today as well as those of the past.
(2 hours, 1 term.)

25. *Seminar in Modern Catholic Literature.*—A seminar in which the students have an opportunity of examining the important phases of the Catholic Literary Revival in England, on the Continent, and in America. Papers, discussions, and occasional lectures.
Prerequisite: Senior or Junior Standing.

30. *Business English.*—A study of the principles of business correspondence, and of their application to the forms of modern business writing. (2 hours, 2 terms.)

FINANCE

James J. Henry, M.A.

1. *Money and Credit.*—The qualities of sound money, the gold standard, money systems of the U. S.; State banking; banking statements and statistics. The Federal Reserve System. Practical problems in modern banking.
(6 hours, 1 term.)

2. *Stock Markets.*—Organization and function of exchanges. Regulations of New York Stock Exchange. Types of dealers and brokers. Contract and orders. Listing and transfer of securities. Methods of buying and selling unlisted securities. Clearing house systems. Nature and use of future contracts. Market news and its transfer. (4 hours, 1 term.)

3. *Corporation Finance.*—Corporate organization in modern business; its legal organization; classification of the instruments of finance; promotion, underwriting, capitalization, earnings, expenses, surplus, insolvency, receivership, reorganization and regulation.
(4 hours, 1 term.)

4. *Investments.*—Markets and their influence on the price of securities. Elements of sound investments and methods of computing earnings, amortization, rights. Government, municipal, railroad, steamship, real estate, street railway, industrial and oil securities as investments.
(4 hours, 1 term.)

[35]

FRENCH
BROTHER E. PIUS, F.S.C., LITT.D.
JOHN GUISCHARD, M.A.

1a. *Elements.*—Introductory grammar.
(3 hours, 1 term.)

1b. *Elements.*—Introductory grammar and reading.
(3 hours, 1 term.)

2. *Review Grammar and Composition.*—Accompanied by readings of selected works. Prerequisites, French 1 or two years of high school French.
(3 hours, 1 term.)

3. *Intermediate Grammar and Composition.*—Accompanied by readings. Prerequisite, French 2.
(3 hours, 1 term.)

4. *The Short Story.*—Reading and interpretation of modern French authors. Prerequisite, French 2, 3.
(2 hours, 1 term.)

5. *Survey of French Literature.*—Selected biographical sketches of authors and excerpts from their works from "La Chanson de Roland" to modern times. Prerequisite, French 2, 3.
(2 hours, 1 term.)

6. *Advanced Composition.*—Exercises in spoken and written French. Intended for those who are majoring in French.
(3 hours, 1 term.)

9. *The Comedies of Molière.*—Prerequisite, French 4, 5.
(2 hours, 1 term.)

11. *French Classical Tragedy.*—Class reading, discussion and reports on Corneille and Racine. Prerequisite, French 4, 5.
(2 hours, 1 term.)

12. *The French Novel.*—The development of the novel in France from the beginning to the end of the nineteenth century; readings and reports. Prerequisite, French 4, 5.
(2 hours, 1 term.)

GERMAN
BROTHER E. ABDON, F.S.C., M.A.

1a. *Elements.*—Introductory German Grammar, first half.
(3 hours, 1 term.)

1b. *Introductory Grammar and Reading,* second half.
(3 hours, 1 term.)

2, 3. *Intermediate Grammar and Composition.*—Intermediate Reading—Class reading and assigned texts to be read out of class. Prerequisite, German 1a and b, or two years of high school German.
(3 hours, 2 terms.)

[36]

4, 5. *Advanced Prose and Dramatic Reading.*—Reading and discussion of selected classics. Prerequisite, German 2, 3.
(2 hours, 2 terms.)

6. *Reading of Scientific Prose.*—Prerequisite, German 2.
(2 hours, 1 term.)

7. *Medical German.*—Prerequisite, German 6. Course restricted to the field of medicine. (2 hours 1 term.)

8. *History of German Literature.*—Lectures one hour throughout the year. Prerequisite, German 5.
(1 hour, 2 terms.)

9. *Nineteenth Century German Drama.*—Lectures and readings of selected works of Kleist, Grillparzer, Hebbel, Hauptmann and other dramatists. Prerequisite, German 5. (3 hours, 1 term.)

11. *Modern German Lyrics.*—Lectures and reading of selected texts. Prerequisite, German 5. (2 hours, 1 term.)

12. *The German Novel of the Nineteenth Century.*—Lectures and readings of selected texts. Prerequisite, German 5.
(2 hours, 1 term.)

13. *Goethe's Faust.*—Lectures on the genesis of the drama and interpretation of the text. Prerequisite, German 8.
(3 hours, 1 term.)

GREEK

Brother D. Thomas, F.S.C., Ph.D.

1. *Elementary Greek.*—Study of forms and syntax. Reading and translation exercises. Prose composition.
(6 hours, 1 term.)

2. *The Anabasis.*—Review of forms and syntax. Selected readings from the Anabasis. Literary background. Prose composition. (3 hours, 1 term.)

4. *Homer: The Iliad.*—Selections. Background readings.
(3 hours, 1 term.)

5. *New Testament.*—Selections from the New Testament. New Testament syntax and vocabulary. Background study.
(3 hours, 1 term.)

6. *The Attic Orators.*—Selections. Especially from Lysias. Not offered 1942-3. (3 hours, 1 term.)

[37]

LA SALLE COLLEGE

HISTORY

Brother D. Augustine, F.S.C., M.A., Ph.D.
Brother D. Thomas, F.S.C., Ph.D.

11. *The Ancient World.*—A brief survey of the oriental civilizations which influenced the Greeks; a study of the more important phases of Greek civilization; a study of the history of Rome from the beginning to the disintegration of the Empire. Particular attention will be given to Roman organizations and administration.

(4 hours, 1 term.)

13. *The Middle Ages* (300 to 1300).—The period between the decline of the Classical World and the emergence of the Modern European. Also a survey of the Arabic-Byzantine Civilization. (4 hours, 1 term.)

14a. *Europe in Transition* (1300 to 1600).—The early history of our West European Culture. The Renaissance and Reformation. (2 hours, 1 term.)

14b. *Modern Europe* (1600 to 1815).—The Age of Great Discoveries in almost all fields. The Expansion of Europe. (2 hours, 1 term.)

15. *Europe Since Napoleon* (1815 to 1935).—The Industrial Revolution, Democracy, Nationalism and Imperialism. The economic, social and cultural problems of a hourgeois society. The World War and the problems it has introduced. (4 hours, 1 term.)

History 14 and 15 given in alternate years.

16. *History of England.*—A general survey of the History of England with particular emphasis on its constitutional evolution. (4 hours, 1 term.)

[38]

20. *United States History.*—Colonial period; origin and development of our institutions; the Revolution; formation and adoption of the Federal Constitution; the social and political life of the period; the Civil War; the reconstruction period; the chief events in domestic politics and foreign relations to the present time.

(4 hours, 1 term.)

21. *Historiography.*—A course intended primarily for history majors. Junior standing will be required. A survey of the great historians of the past and of all the most important historical theories. Research and history teaching will also be discussed.

(4 hours, 1 term.)

23. *History of Civilization.*—A general survey of the cultural achievements of Mankind since pre-historic times. The important cultures will be treated as units.

(4 hours, 1 term.)

24. *Constitutional History of the United States.*—The European, English and American background of the Constitution. The Constitutional Convention of 1787. The Constitution itself. The later growth and interpretations down to the present time.

(4 hours, 1 term.)

INSURANCE

JÁMES J. HENRY, M.A.

1. *Insurance Principles and Practices.*—An elementary course designed to familiarize the student with the fundamental facts of insurance. A survey of (1) the underlying principles (2) practices and (3) legal aspects of life, fire, marine, fidelity and corporate surety, employers' liability, title and credit insurance.

(5 hours, 1 term.)

LATIN

BROTHER D. THOMAS, F.S.C., PH.D.

8. *Prose Composition.*—Disconnected sentences and continuous passages based on Cæsar and Livy. Study of syntax.
(1 hour, 2 terms.)

9. *Cicero.*—Selections from philosophical or oratorical works.
(3 hours, 1 term.)

10. *Livy.*—Selections from book 1, 21, and 22.
Not offered 1942-3. (3 hours, 1 term.)

11. *Latin Epistolography.*—Selections from the letters of Cicero, Pliny and Seneca. Not offered 1942-3.
(3 hours, 1 term.)

12. *Horace.*—Odes and epodes.
(3 hours, 1 term.)

13. *Roman Comedy.*—Selected readings from Plautus and Terence. Background readings.
(3 hours, 1 term.)

15. *Patristic Latin.*—Selections from the Latin Fathers and other early Christian authors.
(3 hours, 1 term.)

16. *Medieval Latin.*—Selections from various authors from the sixth to the nineteenth century. Medieval songs; Christian hymns. (3 hours, 1 term.)

18. *Survey of Classical Latin Literature.*—Selections from classical prose and verse. Background readings.
(3 hours, 1 term.)

19. *Special Latin.*—Study of an author and his works.
(3 hours, 1 term.)

20. *Private Life of The Romans.*—Knowledge of Latin not needed. Readings in English.
(2 hours, 1 term.)

30. *Introductory Philology.*—General principles of language development. Relations of Latin to the Romance languages and to English. Knowledge of Latin not absolutely necessary. Not offered 1942-3.
(1 hour, both terms.)

MATHEMATICS

BROTHER GEORGE LEWIS, F.S.C., M.A., Sc.D.

BROTHER G. JOHN, F.S.C., M.A.

1. *College Algebra.*—Topics covered will include the theory of equations, and combinations, complex numbers, mathematical induction.
(3 hours, 1 term.)

2. *Plane Trigonometry.*—Trigonometric functions, analysis, general values of angles, trigonometric equations.
(3 hours, 1 term.)

3. *Mathematics of Business.*—A course designed to acquaint the students of Business Administration and Law with the fundamentals of the mathematics used in accounting and business practice.
(6 hours, 1 term.)

4. *Analytic Geometry.*—Loci and equations, straight line, circle, conic sections. Prerequisites, M1, M2.
(3 hours, 1 term.)

5. *Plane and Spherical Trigonometry.*—This is a more advanced course than Mathematics 2. It is intended for those Freshmen who studied Plane Trigonometry in high school.
(3 hours, 1 term.)

6. *Differential Calculus.*—Differentiation and applications. Prerequisites, M4.
(3 hours, 1 term.)

7. *Integral Calculus.*—Prerequisite, M6.

(3 hours, 1 term.)

8. *Differential Equations.*—Prerequisites, M6, M7.

(3 hours, 1 term.)

10. *Advanced Calculus.*—Prerequisite, M7.

(3 hours, 1 term.)

MECHANICS

BROTHER GEORGE LEWIS, F.S.C., M.A., Sc.D.

1. *Applied Mechanics.*—A course designed to give a firm grasp of the fundamental principles of Mechanics. Prerequisites, Mathematics 6, 7, and 10.

(3 hours, 1 term.)

3. *Analytic Mechanics.*—Develops the facility of applying the mathematical formulae derived by Calculus and its foundations to the investigation of many forms of physical phenomena. Prerequisites, Mathematics 6 and 7.

(3 hours, 1 term.)

PHILOSOPHY AND PSYCHOLOGY

BROTHER EMILIAN PHILIP, F.S.C., PH.D.

1. *Modern Thomistic Philosophy.*—A comprehensive survey of Neo-Scholastic thought in the fields of Ontology, Cosmology, Philosophy of Mind, Epistemology and Theodicy.

(3 hours, 2 terms.)

2. *Logic.*—A study of the objective though formal conditions of valid inference, and the application of logical principles in all departments of thought. The course is so presented that justice is done to supplementary approaches to logic.

(3 hours, 1 term.)

7. *General Psychology.*—The nervous system. Neural action in relation to consciousness. Sensation. Perception. Memory. Imagination. Reasoning. Instinct. Feeling. Emotions. Action and Willing. Spirituality and immortality of the soul.

(3 hours lecture, 1 term.)

13. *History of Philosophy.*—The development of reasoned human thought from its earliest beginnings to the present time. This course is designed to insert each world-view in its proper setting; to connect it with the intellectual, political, moral, social and religious factors of its present, past and future, and to trace the spiral of progress in the history of human speculation.

A.—From Thales to Meister Eckhart.

(3 hours, 1 term.)

B.—From Hobbes to Bergson. (3 hours, 1 term.)

14. *Psychology of Adjustment.*—A dynamic approach to the problems of an integrated personality, designed to assist the student in his common individual and social adjustments. (3 hours, 1 term.)

PHYSICS

BROTHER G. JOSEPH, F.S.C., M.A.

BROTHER G. JOHN, F.S.C., M.A.

1. *General Physics.* A general course in the fundamentals of physics. Lectures, recitations, problem work, and laboratory in mechanics, heat, sound, light, magnetism and electricity.

(6 hours lecture, 4 hours laboratory, 1 term.)

4. *Geometrical and Physical Optics.*—The principles and methods of geometrical optics. Wave theory of the refraction, dispersion, interference, diffraction, and polar-

ization of light. Experiments with lenses, mirrors, microscopes, spectroscopes, and polariscopes. Applications. Library reports.

(2 hours lecture, 4 hours laboratory, 1 term.)

5. *Thermodynamics.*—The laws of Thermodynamics; Kinetic Theory of Gases; the Quantum Theory; Radiation. Lectures, recitations, and discussions.
Not offered 1942-3. (3 hours, 1 term.)

6. *Electricity and Magnetism.*—The electric field; potential; its measurement; capacitance; current; electromotive force and resistance. Fundamental measurements; thermal and electrical effects of the current; application of thermal effects. Primary and secondary cells; thermoelectric phenomena. Magnetism; magnetic effects of the electric current. Electro-magnetic induction. Alternating currents; transformers; motors. Electrical units; electronics. Roentgen rays; radioactivity; electro-magnetic waves and special applications.

(2 hours lecture, 4 hours laboratory, 1 term.)

7. *Meteorology.*—An introductory course in the basic principles of meteorology; recent advances in weather analysis and forecasting; modern methods for frontal and air-mass analysis. Problems in decoding and plotting weather station synoptic reports.

(3 hours, 1 term.)

9. *Atomic Physics.*—An introductory course in the theory of atomic structure; photoelectric effect; x-rays; atomic spectra, and related topics in the field of modern physics.

(3 hours, 1 term.)

PHYSICAL EDUCATION

JAMES J. HENRY, M.A.

By a program of progressive activities the College hopes to bring healthy students to the peak of physical fitness and to remedy the defects which are caused by lack of physical exercises and poor posture. The physical fitness program includes: calisthenics selected from the U. S. Army and the U. S. Navy Manuals; correct posture instruction; remedial exercises; hiking—one hour each week; supervised games; swimming; riding; intramural contests in: touch football, basketball, softball, bowling, tennis, volley ball, etc.

POLITICAL SCIENCE

BROTHER G. LEONARD, F.S.C., M.A.

1. *American Government.*—The organization and function of the government system of the United States with particular stress on modern problems and political issues. National government.

    (6 hours, 1 term.)

3. *Municipal Administration.*—The functions of cities in the United States; administrative machinery, personnel, methods; public works, city planning, disposal of waste and sewage, health, police protection, fire protection; sources of revenue; expenditure and its checks.

    (2 hours, 1 term.)

4. *American Political Parties.*—Survey of the development of present day political parties; their organization and function; modern tendencies in party alignments.

    (2 hours, 1 term.)

RELIGION

The Course in Religion is designed to present a study of questions and problems which confront the Catholic in his daily life. It presents the Catholic religion as a life to be lived.

1. *Ideal of Catholic Life.*—Love of God and Neighbor; essential and practical duties to God as expressed in the Commandments and demanded by Justice. Our obligations toward our fellow men in the exercise of Charity. (2 hours, 2 terms.)

2. *Motives and Means of Catholic Life.*—Motives: The great Catholic dogmas. Means: Prayer, Grace, The Sacraments and Liturgy. (2 hours, 2 terms.)

3. *Christ and His Church.*—The Study of the life of Christ, His Divinity and His teachings. Structure, functions and practical mission of the Church; relations to science, society and the state. (2 hours, 2 terms.)

4. *Life Problems.*—Faith and spiritual growth; health, leisure and vocational problems; marriage, social and civic activities. (2 hours, 2 terms.)

5. *Special Ethics.*—Man's rights and duties as an individual. Man's duties to God; adoration, love, obedience. Man's duties to his neighbor. Man's rights and duties as a citizen. The common law of nations. Ecclesiastical society. (2 hours, 2 terms.)

6. *Natural Theology.*—Proof of God's existence and providence; Deism, pantheism, agnosticism, atheism. Existence of evil. Preservation of creatures. Divine concurrence. (2 hours, 2 terms.)

SPANISH

BROTHER E. LOUIS, F.S.C., M.A.

1a. *Elements.*—Introductory Spanish Grammar, first half.
(3 hours, 1 term.)

1 b. *Introductory Grammar and Reading,* second half.
(3 hours, 1 term.)

2, 3. *Intermediate Grammar and Composition.*—Intermediate Reading—class reading and assigned texts outside of class. Prerequisite, Spanish 1, a and b, or two years of high school Spanish. (3 hours, 2 terms.)

4, 5. *Advanced Prose Reading.*—Reading and discussion of selected classics. Prerequisite, Spanish 2, 3.
(2 hours, 2 terms.)

6, 7. *Spanish for Commercial Correspondence and Usage.*—Study of commercial Spanish; exercises in Spanish conversation. Prerequisite, Spanish 2, 3.
(2 hours, 2 terms.)

SOCIOLOGY

BROTHER D. AUGUSTINE, F.S.C., M.A., PH.D.

1. *Introduction to Sociology.*—A study of human group life, and the culture of the group. This course is designed as a preparation for the special fields of sociology as well as a general view of courses in this department.
(3 hours, 1 term.)

3. *Social Problems.*—Ignorance, intemperance, vice, unemployment, family maladjustment, special problems of the aged and children. The several agencies, public and private caring for social conditions.
(2 hours, 1 term.)

4. *The Family.*—A study of the environmental factors of family life. Family organization and development. Special stress is laid on the modern problems of divorce and legislation dealing with the family.
(2 hours, 1 term.)

5. *Social Institutions.*—The Church, the State, the School, etc. Their moral and mutual relations. The elements of strength and weakness of all social organizations and their common traits.
(2 hours, 1 term.)

[47]

SCHOLARSHIPS

The Henry T. Coleman Scholarship, founded by the late Henry T. Coleman, Esq., in 1903.

The William F. Harrity Scholarship, founded by the late Honorable William F. Harrity, in 1913.

The Patrick Curran Scholarship, founded in 1914, by Rev. Edward J. Curran, A.M., LL.D., in memory of his father.

Three full scholarships valued at approximately $800 each are offered to the winners of a competitive examination held at the College on the first Saturday of May. A psychological test and examinations in English and Mathematics are the subjects in which the applicant is examined. Students who have graduated from a commercial department and who intend to enter the Business Course at La Salle may substitute for Mathematics an examination in business subjects, including Economics, Law, Accounting and Arithmetic.

Catholic graduates and seniors in an approved secondary school are eligible for the competitive examination.

The following high schools have the privilege of appointing one of the honor graduates to La Salle College:

West Philadelphia Catholic High School
La Salle College High School
Northeast Catholic High School
Roman Catholic High School
Southeast Catholic High School
St. Thomas More High School
St. James High School, Chester
Camden Catholic High School

Lightning Source UK Ltd.
Milton Keynes UK
UKHW020628060119
334855UK00006B/267/P